SCHOOL DAZE

EDITED BY

ARTHUR LIEBERS

Cover Designed By B. Rutherford

SCHOLASTIC BOOK SERVICES

NEW YORK • TORONTO • LONDON • AUCKLAND • SYDNEY • TOKYO

ISBN: 0-590-08094-6

Copyright © 1958 by TAB Books, Inc. This edition is published by Scholastic Book Services, a division of Scholastic Magazines, Inc.

23 22 21 20 19 18 17 16   9/7 0 1 2 3/8
                Printed in U.S.A.   11

CONTENTS

The Ben Roth Agency

"Who burned my report card?"

CLASSROOM CAPERS

The Whole Truth

Willie had just received an "A" for the map of Europe that he had drawn.

"Willie," said his teacher, "this map is excellent! Did anyone help you do it?"

"Oh, no, Miss White," said Willie.

"Come now, tell me the truth. Didn't your father help you?"

"No, Miss White," said Willie, "my father didn't help me. He did it all by himself."

Long Division

Miss Jones was teaching fractions to the class and decided to use a steak as an example.

"If I cut a steak into four parts," she asked, "what do I get?"

"Quarters," answered the class.

"And if I cut those pieces in half?"

"Eighths," answered the class.

"What do I have if I cut those pieces in half again?"

"Sixteenths," replied the class.

"Now suppose I do it once more?" Miss Jones went on. "What do I have then?"

A voice from the back of the room answered firmly, "Hash!"

A Soft Answer

"James, what did you do when Edward called you a liar?" asked the teacher.

"I remembered what you told us, Miss Brown, 'a soft answer turns away anger.'"

"Very good, James! What soft answer did you give him?"

"Why, I hit him with a very soft tomato!"

Shhh!

SUBSTITUTE TEACHER: "Now for the next few minutes I want you all to be so still that you can hear a pin drop."

IMPATIENT IRA: *(After a minute)* "Well, teacher, let it drop!"

Bless You

TEACHER: "Are you doing anything for your cold?"

BENNY: "Why sure, I sneeze whenever it wants me to!"

Ambitious

TEACHER: "Goodness, Gus, haven't you finished washing that blackboard yet? You've been working on it for an hour."

GOOFY GUS: "I know, but the more I wash it, the blacker it gets."

2

Accident

TEACHER: "Walter, how did you get that bump on your head? Have you been fighting again?"

WALTER: "No, teacher."

TEACHER: "Then how did it happen?"

WALTER: "It was an accident."

TEACHER: "An accident?"

WALTER: "Yes, I was sitting on Peter Stone and I forgot to hold his feet."

Horrors!

TEACHER: "Who can give me a sentence with the word 'gruesome' in it?"

SMART SAM: "I can! The man stopped shaving and gruesome whiskers."

End of Week

TEACHER: "Buster Brown, I've had to scold you every day this week. Have you anything to say for yourself?"

BUSTER BROWN: *(With a sigh)* "I'm sure glad it's Friday."

Zip Quip

TEACHER: "Can anyone give me a sentence using the word 'fascinate'?"

BRIGHT BOB: "My sister broke the zipper on her jacket and now she can't fascinate."

On and On

TEACHER: "Jane, please spell 'banana.'"

JANE: "B-a-n-a-n-a—I know how to spell it, Miss Baxter, but I don't know when to stop."

Sure Enough

TEACHER: "What does Brazil produce more of than any other country?"

STAN: *(Quick as a flash)* "Brazilians!"

Helpmates

MISS CARSON: *(Looking over John's homework)* "I don't see how it's possible for one person to make so many mistakes."

JOHN: *(Proudly)* "It wasn't one person, Miss Carson, my father helped me."

Once Done

TEACHER: "Always remember, class, that a job well done need never be done again."

SMALL TIRED VOICE FROM BACK OF ROOM: "What about cutting the grass?"

Unfair

Henry and Herbert had been whispering in back of the room. To teach them a lesson the teacher ordered them to write their names on the board 200 times. Fifteen minutes later Henry came to the teacher and complained:

"This just isn't fair."

"Not fair?" said the teacher.

"No," protested Henry. "His last name is Bly and mine's Pendergastman."

Happy Birthday

TEACHER: "What great event took place in 1809?"

TONY: "Lincoln was born."

TEACHER: "Correct. Now, can anyone tell me what happened in 1812?"

TONY: "Yes, teacher, Lincoln had his third birthday."

Clever Girl

TEACHER: "Suzy, would you rather have one half of an orange or five-tenths of an orange?"

SUZY: *(Quickly)* "Oh, I'd rather have a half."

TEACHER: "Think carefully, Suzy. Why?"

SUZY: "Because you would lose too much juice when you cut the orange into five-tenths!"

It Adds Up

TEACHER: "Jane, if you had three apples and ate one, how many would you have?"

JANE: "Three."

TEACHER: "Three?"

JANE: "Yes, two outside and one inside."

It's O.K. with Freddy

MISS WHITE: (*Annoyed*) "Freddy Jones, I'd like to go through a whole day just once without having to scold you or punish you."

FREDDY: (*Enthusiastically*) "You have my permission, Miss White."

Stage Struck

TEACHER: "Now before we start working on our class play, tell me, have any of you ever had any stage experience?"

SMART SAM: "I had my leg in a cast once."

Construction Job

TEACHER: "Sam, when was Rome built?"

DAVE: "It was built during the night."

TEACHER: "The night! Where did you ever get such an idea?"

DAVE: "Well, everybody knows that Rome wasn't built in a day."

David Pascal, Broadway Laughs

"Our TV set is out of order and everything was so quiet last night I couldn't do my homework."

Stiff Question

TEACHER: "Mary, can you name two foods that contain protein?"

MARY: *(Promptly)* "Eggs and fish."

TEACHER: "Now Danny, name three things containing starch."

DANNY: *(Who has been daydreaming)* "Er-er two cuffs and a collar."

Good Idea

Jane didn't like arithmetic much, but this month she had really worked on it. When report cards were given out the teacher said with a big smile, "Jane, it makes me very happy to be able to give you 80 per cent in arithmetic."

Jane replied eagerly, "Why don't you really enjoy yourself, Miss Smith, and give me 90?"

On One Hand

TEACHER: "If you stood with your back to the north and faced south, what would be on your left hand?"

PETE: *(Quick as a flash)* "Fingers."

Didn't They?

TEACHER: "George Washington was one of our greatest Americans. Can anyone tell us why we honor him?"

EAGER EDGAR: "I know! Because he had a very good memory."

TEACHER: *(Startled)* "Memory?"

EAGER EDGAR: "Why yes, didn't they erect a monument to his memory?"

8

All Gone

Paul always said, "I have went." Finally, after many unsuccessful efforts to correct his grammar, the teacher made Paul stay after school. He had to write on the blackboard one hundred times, "I have gone."

When the teacher returned to the classroom later, she found "I have gone" written all over the blackboard. On her desk was this note: "Dear Teacher: I have written 'I have gone' a hundred times. So now I have went home."

Inside Story

The class was having a composition lesson.

"Do not imitate what other people write," the teacher said. "Simply be yourself and write what is in you."

Following this advice, Tommy Wise turned in the following composition: "We should not imitate others. We should write what is in us. In me there is my stomach, heart, liver, two apples, one piece of pie, a lemon drop, and my lunch."

Fish Story

SOCIAL STUDIES TEACHER: "When the Eskimos trade, they use fish instead of money."

ARTIE: *(Thoughtfully)* "They must have an awful time getting gum out of a slot machine."

The class was discussing the shape of the earth. To prove that it was round, the teacher said to Tom: "Your father is a sailor. If he kept on sailing in the same direction, wouldn't he come back to his starting point?"

"No, Miss Cameron."

"No, Tom? Why not?"

"Because he works on a ferry."

❂ ❂ ❂

MISS WINN: "Steve, I wish you wouldn't whistle while you are studying."

STEVE: "I wasn't studying, Miss Winn, just whistling."

Short and Sweet

TEACHER: "Billy, why is it that everyone else has at least a five-page report on 'milk,' and your composition is only a half page?"

BILLY: "Well, you see, I was writing about condensed milk."

Building Business for Pop

MISS RYAN: (*To Paul whose father is a doctor*) "Paul, if your work doesn't improve I think it will be necessary for me to call on your father."

PAUL: (*Politely*) "That will be fine, Miss Ryan. His office hours are three to five, and his fee is five dollars a visit."

10

Good Answer

TEACHER: "If you added 500, 38, 64 and 53, and divided that by 35, what would you get?"

MARGIE: *(Dazed)* "The wrong answer."

© Creaciones Editoriales, The Ben Roth Agency

"You're feeding him too much Geography!"

Be Prepared

HOME ECONOMICS TEACHER: "Why should every room in your house always be clean, in order, and well-aired?"

JOAN: "Because you never know when company may drop in."

One Reason

TEACHER: "Why should we do all we can to prevent war?"

HOMER: "It makes too much history for us to learn."

Barnyard Chatter

TEACHER: "Among our spelling words for today is the word 'hence.' Wilbur, can you give me a sentence using the word 'hence'?"

WILBUR: "Hence are female chickens."

Try This for Size

TEACHER: "I'm afraid this desk is a little too small for you, Tom."

TALL TOM: "Don't worry about it. I'll add two feet to it when I sit down."

Big Wind

TEACHER: "Can anyone tell me why hurricanes are named after girls?"

MIKE: (In a whisper) "Did you ever hear of a 'himmicane'?"

Short Count

Little Richard came back into class after recess period with a bleeding nose and a badly scratched face.

"So you've been fighting again," the teacher reprimanded him. "Haven't I asked you to count to a hundred before doing anything when you are angry?"

"Yes," Richard admitted, "but the other boy's teacher must have told him to count to ten."

❀ ❀ ❀

TEACHER: "Albert, can you name a bird that is now extinct?"

ALBERT: "Yes, Miss French, our canary. The cat extincted him last night."

Achoo!

MISS BELL: "Henry, I notice that you're still coughing and sneezing. Are you taking any medicine for your cold?"

HENRY: "I'm trying to, Miss Bell, but I just can't."

MISS BELL: "And why can't you?"

HENRY: "The doctor gave me some pills, and on the bottle it says 'one pill to be taken three times a day.' Now no matter how hard I try, I can't take a pill more than once."

Test Day

I love exams,
I think they're fun.
I never study,
I never fail one—
(I'm the teacher!)

One + One

TEACHER: "George, if Dave gave you a dog and Jane gave you a dog, how many dogs would you have?"
GEORGE: "Four."
TEACHER: "Now, George, think carefully before you answer. How could you have four when Dave gave you one and Jane gave you one?"
GEORGE: "Because I already have two dogs."

Overworked

The teacher had asked Eddie to put plastic covers on some books in the class library. She came back about an hour later and asked: "Eddie, how many books have you covered?"

Eddie answered brightly, "When I finish the one I'm working on and another, I'll have two."

Menu

TEACHER: "What insect requires the least food?"
DONALD: "A moth. It lives on holes."

14

Chas. Skiles, The Ben Roth Agency

"I'm afraid an apology is called for, Miss Bramble. I checked his excuse, and there WAS a lion in their bathroom this morning!"

Tick Tock

Have you heard about the sign on a classroom wall? "TIME PASSES—WILL YOU?"

Horse Sense

TEACHER: "Looie, I asked you to draw a horse and wagon. You've only drawn a horse."

LOOIE: "I figured the horse would draw the wagon."

15

Honest Answer

TEACHER: "Joey, if you had five pieces of candy and Tony asked you for one, how many pieces would you have left?"
JOEY: "Five."

Double Talk

TEACHER: "Class, we'll have only a half day of school this morning."
JOHNNY: "Hooray!"
TEACHER: "Quiet please, we'll have the other half this afternoon."

* * *

BILL: "How did you do on your history test?"
JOE: "Well, er, you see, it was like this . . ."
BILL: "Yeah, I failed, too."

Stretching It

JOHNNY: (*On a class walk*) "Teacher, did you see that great big car go by. It was as big as a house!"
TEACHER: "Johnny, why must you exaggerate so much. I've told you at least 40 million times to correct that terribly bad habit of yours."

MISS MYERS: *(To new class)* "Now children, when I call on you I'd like you to tell the class your name. Will the boy in the first seat tell us his name?"

PUPIL: "My name is Julie."

MISS MYERS: "In this class we use our full names, not nicknames. Your name is Julius." Turning to second boy, "And what is your name?"

SECOND PUPIL: *(Hesitatingly)* "Well, I guess my name is Billious."

The Sad Truth

Experience is a teacher,
But here's what makes me burn,
She's always teaching me the things
I do not care to learn.

* * *

MISS WILSON: "James, what is the opposite of misery?"

JAMES: "Happiness."

MISS WILSON: "Correct. What is the opposite of sadness?"

JAMES: "Gladness."

MISS WILSON: "Right again. What is the opposite of woe?"

JAMES: "Giddap."

17

Jimmy had trouble pronouncing the letter "R," so his teacher gave him this sentence to practice at home: *Robert gave Richard a rap in the ribs for roasting the rabbit so rare.*

A few days later the teacher asked him to say the sentence for her. Said Jimmy, *"Bob gave Dick a poke in the side for not cooking the bunny enough."*

❖ ❖ ❖

Herbie studied one of the questions on the examination paper long and earnestly. It read: "State the number of tons of coal shipped out of the United States in any given year."

Then his face brightened, and he wrote: "In 1492—none."

❖ ❖ ❖

TEACHER: "If you had ten potatoes and had to divide them equally among twelve people, how would you do it?"

MARGIE: "I'd mash them."

❖ ❖ ❖

TEACHER: "Who can tell me the names of some shooting stars?"

Judy: "I can! Gene Autry, Hopalong Cassidy, and Roy Rogers!"

18

NATURE NONSENSE

A cabbage, a tomato, and a faucet had a race. Can you figure out how they finished?

ANSWER: The cabbage came in ahead; the tomato couldn't catch up; and the faucet is still running.

Moon-Struck

TEACHER: "Walter, which is most useful to us, the sun or the moon?"

WALTER: "The moon, I think."

TEACHER: "Why the moon?"

WALTER: "Because the moon shines at night when we need the light, but the sun is out during the bright light of day."

❋ ❋ ❋

There should be no monotony,
In studying your botany.
It helps to train
And spur your brain—
Unless you haven't got any.

Bird Sense

The class had been discussing the migration of birds.

TEACHER: *(Holding up a picture of an Auk)* "Now, can someone tell me where this bird comes from?"

VOICE FROM THE BACK OF THE ROOM: "From an egg!"

❋ ❋ ❋

SMART: "Can you make up a poem using the words 'analyze' and 'anatomy'?"

ALECK: "Sure! How's this?

> My analyze over the ocean,
> My analyze lies over the sea
> My analyze over the ocean
> Oh bring back my anatomy."

Small Wonder

TEACHER: "Birds, though small, are remarkable creatures. For example, what can a little bird do that I cannot do?"

WALLY: "Take a bath in a saucer."

Antics

TEACHER: "What can you tell me about ants that shows how intelligent they are?"

ALERT ALFRED: "They always find the place where people are having a picnic."

Miss Alden had been describing the wonders of the human body to her class. Using a skeleton, she showed them how the joints worked, and gave them the names of some of the larger bones.

After lunch she proceeded to review the lesson. "How many bones are there in your body, Tommy?" she asked.

"About nine hundred I guess," replied Tommy promptly.

"Nine hundred!" said Miss Alden, amazed. "You know you can't possibly find nine hundred bones in this skeleton."

"Well, he didn't have sardines for lunch," answered Tommy quickly.

A Bit Fuzzy

TEACHER: "Can anyone in this class explain just what a caterpillar is?"

BERT: (*Confidently*) "A caterpillar is an upholstered worm."

Exit?

TEACHER: "What is bacteria?"

BOB: (*Not quite sure*) "The back entrance to a cafeteria?"

21

An Average Hen

MISS BROWN: "Henry, explain to the class what an 'average' is."

HENRY: "An average is what a hen lays eggs on."

MISS BROWN: "Henry, where did you ever get that idea?"

HENRY: "I read it in a book."

MISS BROWN: "Will you bring that book to school tomorrow?"

HENRY: "Yes, Miss Brown."

The Next Day

HENRY: *(Reading from the book)* "The domestic hen lays on an average of fifty eggs each year."

❋　❋　❋

MISS NORTON: "The fleas we find on domestic animals are small, dark-colored pests."

DANNY: *(Surprised)* "Gee, Miss Norton, I thought fleas were white."

MISS NORTON: "Why, Danny?"

DANNY: "I read a poem once that said 'Mary had a little lamb . . . with fleece as white as snow.'"

MISS SAXTON: "Are there any colors you can actually touch?"

SUE: "Oh, yes, Miss Saxton, I've often felt blue."

❋ ❋ ❋

Herb Green, The Ben Roth Agency

"OK, how was that again . . . if Jim has 45 apples and John has 32 . . .?"

The class had been talking about the frozen Arctic and the animals that live there.

"Joe," asked the teacher, "why does a polar bear wear a fur coat?"

JOE: *(Who had been daydreaming, answered quickly)* "I guess it's much too cold up there to wear a tweed jacket!"

Spelling Bee

TEACHER: "Dick, how did you get that horrible swelling on your nose?"

DICK: "I bent down to smell a brose in my garden."

TEACHER: "There's no 'b' in rose."

DICK: "There was in this one."

Well, Are They?

HANK: "Say, Frank, what are these holes in the wood?"

FRANK: "They are knotholes."

HANK: "Well, if they're not holes, what are they?"

Gulp!

TEACHER: *(During lesson on birds)* "Can anyone tell me where the home of the swallow is?"

FREDDY: "It must be in the stomach."

Quick Change

TEACHER: "Judy, what is your favorite flower?"
JUDY: "Chrysanthemums."
TEACHER: "Spell it, Judy."
JUDY: "I just changed my mind, Miss White, I like roses much better."

Biting Talk

TEACHER: *(After a long lesson on the care of the teeth)* "Now, Kate, name the three kinds of teeth."
KATE: "Temporary, permanent and false."

* * *

JILL: "What's flat at the bottom, pointed at the top, and has ears?"
BILL: "I give up."
JILL: "A mountain."
BILL: "Oh, yeah, what about the ears?"
JILL: "Haven't you ever heard of mountaineers?"

* * *

TEACHER: "Arthur, why does a moth eat holes in rugs?"
ARTHUR: "Maybe it wants to see the floor show."

25

MARY: "Look, you have little white things in your head that bite!"

MOE: *(Excited)* "What little white things? Where?"

MARY: "Your teeth, of course."

✻ ✻ ✻

"Now, Charles," said the teacher. "To what family does the whale belong?"

"I don't know," said Charles rather puzzled. "No family in our neighborhood has one."

✻ ✻ ✻

GOOFY GUS: "Teacher, did you say that when people began using petroleum for lighting lamps they stopped using whale oil?"

TEACHER: "Yes, I did say that, Gus."

GOOFY GUS: "Gosh, what did the whales do for a living after that?"

✻ ✻ ✻

Miss White's class was taking a nature walk and came upon a tiny baby bird breaking out of his shell.

"Is there any question about this miracle of nature that we are watching?" asked Miss White.

Susy spoke up timidly, "Miss White, I see how the little bird gets out of the shell, but what I can't understand is how he got into it."

The first day of school the teacher was proudly showing the class the plants that she had brought in to decorate the classroom. "This," she said, pointing to a pretty flowering plant, "belongs to the Begonia family."

"Can we keep it or do we have to give it back to them?" asked Alice quickly.

*   *   *

WEE WILLIE: "I would like ten cents' worth of bird seed.

CLERK: "How many birds do you have, sonny?"

WEE WILLIE: "None, but I want to grow some."

*   *   *

SPORT TIME SPOOFS

Kickoff

JEAN: "Oh, come on! Why don't they play instead of standing there arguing with the referee?"

JILL: "Don't get excited. We're winning the game that way."

JEAN: "How's that?"

JILL: "Well, Jack told me that our team would win by kicking."

Slow Poke

TONY: (*Eagerly, after running 100 yards*) "How did I do, Coach? Did you take my time?"

COACH: (*Disgusted*) "I didn't have to. You took it yourself."

Take Cover!

TED: "Did you hear that our football team has been recovered?"

FRED: "Really? I didn't know it was lost."

TED: "It wasn't, they got new uniforms."

SPORT TIME SPOOFS

Feet First

GYM TEACHER: "You, there, mark time."

HOMER: "With my feet, sir?"

GYM TEACHER: "Have you ever known anything to mark time with its hands?"

HOMER: "Yes, sir, a clock."

The Ben Roth Agency

"The purpose of the fire drill, Leroy, is to develop teamwork, not individual heroes."

Pie-Proof

"Excuse me," said meek Merton to the big football player in the school cafeteria, "but I think you are sitting on my seat."

"Oh, yeah," growled the football player, "can you prove it?"

"I think so," said Merton. "I left my pie and ice cream on the seat."

Free for All?

GYM TEACHER: "John, who gave you that black eye?"

JOHN: "Nobody gave it to me, sir. I had to fight for it."

Off Base

NATE: "Gosh, look, we have a man on every base."
KATE: "So what? So does the other team."

Time to Duck

SWIMMING INSTRUCTOR: "And another reason for practicing your swimming is that swimming is good for the figure."

VOICE FROM BACK OF THE ROOM: "Did you ever see a duck?"

Batter Up

JIM: "Mary White would make a good baseball player."

TIM: "And why would she make a good baseball player?"

JIM: "A fly got into the bowl when she was making pancakes, and you should have seen how she caught that fly from the batter!"

Bright Idea

BILL: "Ouch, this liniment makes my arm smart."

PHIL: "Why don't you put some on your head?"

❋   ❋   ❋

SOCIAL STUDIES TEACHER: "Where are the biggest diamonds found?"

WISE WINNIE: "In baseball parks!"

❋   ❋   ❋

JUNIOR: "I went out for end on the football team."

DAD: "Didn't make it, huh?"

JUNIOR: "No. I thought I was going to, though. The first day at practice, the coach took one look at me and said, 'Oh, brother, this is the end!'"

"Gloomy Gertie just has no style," complained a classmate.

"How come?" asked another.

"Well! Did you see those baseball stockings she wore all last week?"

"*Baseball* stockings?"

"Yes! They had four runs in them."

*　*　*

COACH: "Johnny, I'll let you be end, guard and tackle."

JOHNNY: "How will you do that?"

COACH: "I'll let you sit at the end of the bench, guard the water bucket, and tackle anybody that gets close to it."

*　*　*

LENNY: "Do you know what is the quietest game played?"

PENNY: "No, what?"

LENNY: "Bowling—you can hear a pin drop."

*　*　*

JOE: "Did you have any luck on your hunting trip?"

MOE: "I'll say I did. I shot 17 geese."

JOE: "Were they wild?"

MOE: "No, but the lady who owned them was!"

MIKE: "Can't you play tennis without making so much noise?"

MEG: "Don't be silly. Who ever heard of playing tennis without raising a racket."

❀   ❀   ❀

GOOFY GIGGLES

Testing

The class was in the middle of their first lesson on baking a cake.

"Mary," said Miss Miller, "please go into the kitchen and see if our cake is done yet. Just stick a knife in the cake and see if it comes out clean."

In a few minutes Mary was back. "Oh, Miss Miller, the knife came out so clean," she said excitedly, "that I stuck in all the other dirty knives too!"

Punishment

Ruth was telling her family about the home economics class.

"Do they let you eat what you prepare?" asked her mother.

"*Let* us?" answered Ruth, "they *make* us!"

No Way Out

It happened in the school cafeteria:

ALICE: (*Opening her lunch box*) "Ugh! I hate cream-cheese-and-jelly sandwiches, and every single day I get the same thing for lunch."

JEAN: "Why don't you tell your mother you don't want cream-cheese-and-jelly sandwiches?"

ALICE: *(Sadly)* "Nope. That wouldn't work. I always make my own sandwiches."

Alas!

JOAN: "Did the people in the audience cry when I died in the second act?"
JACK: "Naw, they knew you were only acting."

❋ ❋ ❋

TEACHER: "Can anyone tell me what makes the Tower of Pisa lean."
KNOW-IT-ALL-NED: "It must be on a diet!"

❋ ❋ ❋

Tch, Tch!

Violets are blue,
You'd be too.
The test was over,
Before I was through.

❋ ❋ ❋

HARRY: "Do you know why Hank sprinkled grass seed all over himself?"
LARRY: "No, why?"
HARRY: "He wanted to be a-lawn."

LOU: "Why do they call that girl 'postscript'?"
SUE: "Because her real name is Adeline More."

* * *

JANE: *(Showing off the cake she has just baked)*
"Look! this is the best thing I've done in cooking class
this year."
JILL: "Don't let that discourage you, dear."

A Matter of Manners

TEACHER: "Vicky, can you tell me what is wrong
with this sentence: 'The horse and cow is in the field.'"
VICKY: "Yes. Ladies should come first."

Crash Program

It had been a trying day for Mrs. Wheatley, the
cooking teacher. The girls in the class had been
dropping dishes like leaves in the fall. Now Ruth and
Rita were cleaning up.

Suddenly there was another loud crash in the pantry.

"More dishes, girls?" asked Mrs. Wheatley in exas-
peration.

"No," came a sweet voice from the pantry, "fewer
dishes."

* * *

The class was visiting a western museum. Wally,
who had once ridden a horse, was showing off his

superior knowledge. "See that long rope hanging from the cowboy's saddle?" he said to Daisy. "The cowboy uses that to catch cows."

"Oh, really," said Daisy, greatly impressed. "And what does he use for bait?"

Nothing Doing

Little Larry came home from his first day at school. "What did you learn, son?" asked his mother.

"Nothing," replied Larry.

"Now Larry, you must have done *something*."

"The only thing that happened," answered Larry, "was that a woman wanted to know how to spell 'cat,' so I told her."

Heavy Number

It was Bobbie's first day at school and Miss Jones asked him the number of his house.

"I don't know, Miss Jones," said Bobbie.

"Tomorrow morning, bring the number of your house to school," instructed Miss Jones.

The next morning Miss Jones said, "Bobbie, have you brought me your house number?"

"No," replied Bobbie. "It was fastened on the door so tightly, I couldn't get it off."

Mary had a little lamb,
A little pork, a little jam,
A little egg on toast,
A little potted roast,
A little stew with dumpling white,
A little shad—
For Mary had
A little appetite.

❋ ❋ ❋

EDDIE: "Edna, did you know it's impossible to send mail to Washington now?"

EDNA: "No, why?"

EDDIE: "Because he's dead. But you can send mail to Lincoln."

EDNA: "How come? He's dead, too."

EDDIE: "I know, but he left his 'Gettysburg Address.'"

❋ ❋ ❋

JOE: "If it takes a man an hour to walk four miles, how long does it take a fly to get through a jar of molasses?"

MOE: (After thinking hard) "I'm stuck."

JOE: "So is the fly."

FAMILY FUNNIES

Making History

JAMES: *(Returning from school)* "Hey, mom, I'm just like Washington, Jefferson and Lincoln."
MOTHER: "How's that?"
JAMES: "I went down in history."

Command Performance

"Say, mom," said Steve. "There's a special P.T.A. meeting at school this afternoon."

"Really?" said his mother. "What's so special about it?"

"It's just for you, my teacher, and the principal—and I've been invited, too."

What's In a Name?

JOHN: "Mother, can't you give me another name?"
MOTHER: "Why, what's wrong with 'John'?"
JOHN: "The teacher keeps saying that she'll keep me after school as sure as my name is John."

Bob Brown walked into the neighborhood grocery store one afternoon with a long shopping list in his hand.

"What can I do for you, young man?" said the grocer.

"Thirteen pounds of coffee at 98 cents a pound," Bob read from his list. "Then I want twenty-nine pounds of sugar at twenty-two cents a pound, five pounds of tea at fifteen cents, two eight-pound hams at eighty-three cents a pound, and five dozen jars of pickles at twenty-one cents a jar. Now, what does that add up to?"

"That's quite an order, Bob," said the grocer. "Let's see . . . it comes to exactly forty-five dollars and seventy-five cents. Do you have the money or did your mother say to charge it?"

"Neither," said Bob, heading for the door. "Thanks a lot—that was my arithmetic homework!"

✹ ✹ ✹

MOTHER: (*To Jean, who is helping her clean house*) "Why aren't you using the vacuum cleaner?"

JEAN: "But mother, I don't have a vacuum to clean."

The Winner

UNCLE FRED: "Tom, who is the most popular boy in your class?"

TOM: "Walter Blake is. Last month he gave us all measles, and we had two weeks off from school."

DAD: "Well, Dan, did you make any mistakes in school today?"

DAN: "Yes, I gave the right answer after Mickey Sullivan gave the wrong answer."

DAD: "But that wasn't a mistake."

DAN: "Yes it was. After school he licked me for doing it."

A Thorough Lad

MRS. WILTON: "Tell me, Mrs. Barclay, how is your son Wilbur getting along in school?"

MRS. BARCLAY: "Oh, just fine. He's so accurate and thorough that he stays in every class for two years."

Right or Wrong

As usual, Terry was having trouble with his arithmetic homework. He chewed up three pencils, and sat through two television programs without getting anything on paper. At last he turned to his father. "Pop," he pleaded. "I wish you'd do this arithmetic problem for me."

After thinking a moment, his father said: "You know son, if I did this problem for you, it just wouldn't be right."

"Maybe it wouldn't," said Terry. "But you could try."

SCHOOL DAZE

No Cause for Alarm

FATHER: "I'm a little worried, son, about your being at the foot of the class."

JUNIOR: "Don't worry, Pop. They teach the same stuff at both ends."

It's the Season

Louise came home in January with a poor report card.

"Well, what happened?" demanded her father.

"You know how it is, Dad," explained Louise. "Everything is marked down after the holidays."

That's Different

MOTHER: *(Looking over Jack's shoulder while he is doing his homework)* "Your spelling is perfectly terrible."

JACK: "That's all right. This isn't a spelling lesson, it's a composition."

A Hair-Raiser

HERBERT: "Hey, Mom, is that hair tonic in the yellow bottle in the medicine chest?"

MOTHER: "No, Herbert, that's glue."

HERBERT: "No wonder I couldn't get my hat off when I got to school this morning."

SOS

Mike was attending boarding school and found himself running very short of money. He proceeded to send his family the following telegram: "Send funds."

The family telegramed this answer to Mike: "What for?"

And Mike simply replied: "For Mike."

Dick Cavalli, Collier's

"It was easy. I just raised my hand and asked if I could leave the room, and here I am."

One's Enough

Rita came home from school and told her mother, "My teacher takes an interest in me. Today she asked me whether I had any younger sisters or brothers, and I told her I am an only child."

"How nice," said her mother, "and what did the teacher say to that?"

Rita replied, "She said, 'Thank goodness.'"

* * *

BIG BROTHER: *(To little sister)* "All right. I'll help you with your homework. Now look, if you had five apples and I took one, how many would you have left?"

LITTLE SISTER: *(Confused)* "I don't know. In my class we do arithmetic with oranges."

First Place

The Jones children were trying to impress their visiting Uncle Dave. All proudly claimed to be first in something. Bobby said he was first in arithmetic; Sally said she won every spelling bee; Walter claimed to be best in social studies. Only little Jane was silent.

"Aren't you first in anything, Jane?" asked Uncle Dave.

"Well," replied Jane thoughtfully, "I'm usually the first one out of the class when the bell rings."

Shhhhh!

SPOILED SON: "Poppa, buy me a drum, I want to play in the school band."

FATHER: "But don't you think it would be rather noisy to have you practicing the drum in the house, son?"

SON: "Oh, no, I'll only practice when you're asleep, Pop."

Good News

FRESHMAN FREDDY: "Dad, you're really in luck!"

FATHER: "What happened?"

FRESHMAN FREDDY: "You won't have to buy any new books for me this year. I'm taking last year's work over again."

❈ ❈ ❈

The bobby-soxer played a new be-bop recording on the phonograph. Turning to her father, who had settled down comfortably to read the evening paper, she exclaimed: "Oh-o-o, have you ever heard anything like it?"

He looked up and replied: "Not really, dear. The closest thing to it I ever heard was when a truck loaded with empty cans ran into a truck full of hogs."

SON: "Pop, will you help me find the least common denominator in this problem?"

POP: "Good heavens, son, don't tell me that hasn't been found—they were looking for it when I was a kid."

*　*　*

Mr. and Mrs. Smith had given Willie a bicycle and were watching proudly as he rode around and around the block.

On his first circuit, Willie shouted: "Look, Mom, no hands."

The second time around: "Look, Mom, no feet."

And the third time: "Look, Mom, no teeth!"

*　*　*

DAD: "There's something wrong with my shaving brush."

DAN: "That's funny. It was all right yesterday when I painted my bicycle."

*　*　*

SAPPY SCIENCE

Inner Space

(A Warning to Young Scientists)

I shot a missile in the air,
It fell to earth, I knew not where,
Until next day, with rage profound,
The man it fell on came around.
In less time than it takes to tell,
He showed me where that missile fell;
And now I do not greatly care
To shoot more missiles in the air.

❀   ❀   ❀

The class was taking a trip to the locomotive works.
"What is that thing?" asked Joan, pointing to a big
piece of equipment.

"That's an engine boiler," replied the man who was
showing them through the plant.

"Why do they boil engines?" asked Joan.

"To make the engine tender," replied the guide.

Person to Person

"Many scientists believe that there is life on other planets," said the teacher, "and someday they believe we might even exchange messages with them. Suppose that the people on Mars send us a message, how could they tell whether we received it?"

To this, little Louie answered brightly: "They might send it collect and see if we paid for it."

Speedway

BEN: "Isn't it fantastic! Just think light travels at the rate of 186,000 miles a second!"

BETTY: "So what? It's downhill all the way."

Catch Your Breath

TEACHER: "Every day we breathe oxygen. What do we breathe at night?"

SARA: "Nitrogen?"

● ● ●

MISS BAKER: "Now we all know that it's the law of gravity that keeps us on this earth."

SALLY: "Well then, Miss Baker, what kept people on earth before the law was passed?"

Stanley & Janice Berenstain, Collier's

"It's not hard to join. You just have to get some adult to sign your card so if you lost any books, they'll have somebody to put in jail."

Strike Out!

MISS REED: "Is it true, Andy, that lightning never strikes twice in the same place?"

ANDY: "Yes, Miss Reed. When lightning strikes once, the same place isn't there any more."

Ups and Downs

GEORGE: "Miss Glenn, if the earth goes round and round, what holds it up?"

MISS GLENN: "The earth circles around the sun, and the sun holds the earth in its orbit by gravitation. Do you understand that?"

GEORGE: "Yes, Miss Glenn, but what holds the earth up when the sun goes down?"

❂ ❂ ❂.

TEACHER: "What is usually used as a conductor of electricity?"

SAMMY: "Why—er—"

TEACHER: "Correct, wire. Now tell me, what is the unit of electrical power?"

SAMMY: "The what?"

TEACHER: "That's absolutely right, the watt."

Junior Birdsmen

Paul was finishing his report to the class on jet aviation. "Our modern fliers can do anything that a bird can do, and more," he announced proudly.

From a corner of the room, Pete whispered: "I'd like to see one sleeping on a telephone wire with his head tucked under his wing!"

It's Paneful

HANK: "Did you hear how Tony got in trouble with Miss Wilcox today?"

HOMER: "No, what happened?"

HANK: "She asked him to name an invention by which we can take pictures through walls."

HOMER: "Well?"

HANK: "He answered, 'a window.'"

Cause and Effect

SCIENCE TEACHER: "Let's assume that I want to switch the electric light on and it doesn't work. What may be wrong?"

SMART ALECK: "Maybe you forgot to pay the bill."

Take a Deep Breath

MISS BROWN: "Without oxygen, human life would be impossible. This important gas was discovered in 1773."

BERNIE: "Miss Brown, what did people breathe before oxygen was discovered?"

The Hazards of Science

A green little chemist,
  On a green little day,
Mixed some green little chemicals,
  In a green little way.
The green little grasses,
  Now tenderly wave,
O'er the green little chemist's,
  Green little grave.

❖ ❖ ❖

TEACHER: "Who was the smartest inventor of all times and why?"

HARRY: "Edison. He invented the phonograph and radio so people would stay up all night using his electric light bulbs."

❖ ❖ ❖

SCIENCE TEACHER: "This gas is deadly poison. What steps would you take if it escaped?"

WILBUR: *(Quickly)* "Long ones, sir."

❖ ❖ ❖

DAFFYNITIONS

TEACHER: "Albert, what is a grudge?"
ALBERT: "A grudge is where you keep automobiles."

❊   ❊   ❊

TEACHER: "Anonymous means, 'without a name.' Now write me a sentence using that word."
AND KENNY WROTE: "Our new baby is anonymous."

❊   ❊   ❊

TEACHER: "What is a widower?"
JOEY: "Why a widower must be the husband of a widow."

❊   ❊   ❊

TEACHER: "When were the so-called dark ages?"
TILLY: "During the days of the knights."

TEACHER: "John, what is sawdust?"

JOHN: *(Thinking hard)* "Oh, yes, it's the past tense of see dust."

❀ ❀ ❀

KEN: "What makes a potato taste bad when you don't put it on?"

BEN: "Salt."

❀ ❀ ❀

TEACHER: "Can someone explain what snoring is?"

KATEY: "Letting off sleep."

❀ ❀ ❀

SUE: "What's mud with the juice squeezed out?"

STU: "Dust."

❀ ❀ ❀

TEACHER: "Billy, can you tell the class just exactly what ice is?"

BRIGHT BILLY: "Oh yes, that's water that stays out in the cold and goes to sleep."

❀ ❀ ❀

NAN: "What do you call someone who can't keep his balance on the the bus?"

FRAN: "A Laplander."

DAFFYNITIONS

Successful Farming

"About this original composition of yours that begins, 'Fourscore and seven years ago ...' "

* * *

NORA: "What's colorless, wet, and turns dark when you wash it?"
NED: "Water."

* * *

TEACHER: "What's in water that puts out fires?"
ANNIE: "A fire boat?"

* * *

TEACHER: "What is etiquette, Jean?"
JEAN: "Etiquette is the noise you don't make when you eat soup."

Ask your teacher this one: "If fortification means a large fort, why doesn't ratification mean a large rat?"

* * *

TEACHER: "What is the plural of man, Johnny?"
JOHNNY: "Men."
TEACHER: "Correct, and what is the plural of child?"
JOHNNY: "Twins."

* * *

TEACHER: "What is an autobiography?"
HUEY: "Er—the life story of an automobile."

* * *

ALIBI: The legal way of proving that a man was not at a place where he really was.

* * *

CAULIFLOWER: A cabbage with a college education.

* * *

CELEBRITY: One who works all his life to become famous enough to be recognized—and then goes around in dark glasses so no one will know who he is.

* * *

CIRCLE: A round straight line with a hole in the middle.

COAL: A purchase which goes not only to the buyer but to the cellar.

* * *

COOKBOOK: Contains many stirring chapters.

* * *

DEPTH: Height turned upside down.

* * *

DIMPLE: A bump inside out.

* * *

FLIRT: A girl who got the guy you tried to get.

* * *

GARLIC: A vegetable whose best friends won't tell it.

* * *

HIGHBROW: One who knows more than he can understand.

* * *

INDISTINCT: Where people put the dirty dishes.

* * *

ITCHES: When a recruit is standing at attention his nose always does.

MOVIES: The place where people talk behind your back.

* * *

RUSSIAN DANCING: This consists of folding one's arms over the chest and running while sitting down.

* * *

SNEEZE: The explosion of a tickle.

* * *

STEAM: Water gone crazy with the heat.

* * *

SYNONYM: The word you use when you don't know how to spell the one you want to use.

* * *

TELEGRAM: The only place where words, not deeds, count.

* * *

TROUSERS: An uncommon noun, singular at the top and plural at the bottom.

DAFFYNITIONS

QUESTION: "What is a hot dog?"
ANSWER: "A hot dog is the noblest of all dogs, because it feeds the hand that bites it."

❊ ❊ ❊

A man asked his wife if she knew what radar was.
"Of course," she answered. "Radar is something that when it's foggy outside the airplane lands anyhow."

❊ ❊ ❊

QUICK QUIPS.

JANE: "Have you kept up with your studies?"
JOAN: "Yes, but I haven't passed them."

* * *

UNCLE DAN: "Willie, which side of Broad Street is your school on?"
WILLIE: "Both."
UNCLE DAN: "How can that be?"
WILLIE: "It all depends. If you're going up Broad Street, it's on the left; and if you're coming down the street, it's on the right."

Greedy

LITTLE LUCY: "A half pint of chocolate milk, please."
COUNTER CLERK: "Want to drink it here or take it with you?"
LITTLE LUCY: "Both."

QUICK QUIPS

The Morning After

MISS BLAKE: "You missed my class yesterday, didn't you, Aleck?"

ALECK: "Not at all, Miss Blake."

Help!

Charlie was failing fifth grade. He went to a college student to see whether he would help him with his studies.

"All right," said the college student, "I'll be glad to help you. I'll charge you twelve dollars for the first month, and six dollars for the second month."

"That's fine," said Charlie, after thinking it over. "I'll come the second month."

Same Channel

TV STAR: *(To his son)* "Were you promoted?"

SON: "Promoted! I was held over for another 26 weeks!"

* * *

ANN: "Sam, you don't look too well today. How do you feel?"

SAM: "Well, I have a slight cold."

ANN: "Have you a temperature?"

SAM: "No, the school nurse took it."

61

Inspiration

The principal was speaking to the school assembly. "Always remember," he said "that whatever you attempt, there is only one way to learn and that is to begin at the bottom. There are no exceptions to this rule."

A loud whisper from the back of the room asked, "What about swimming?"

A B C's

BEN: "Al is the first person you learn about when you start in school."
KEN: "Al who?"
BEN: "Alphabet."

Three Little Words

MAGGIE: "What are the three words most often used by students in school?"
MOE: "I don't know."
MAGGIE: "Correct."

It's the Truth

Did you hear about the pupil who said, "Words fail me," as he flunked a spelling test?

Generous

TEACHER: "Unselfishness is giving up willingly something that you need. Can you give me an example of unselfishness, Johnny?"

JOHNNY: "I go without a bath when I need one."

Impossible?

CAROL: "If an empty barrel weighed 30 pounds, what could you fill it with to make it weigh 28 pounds?"

CHARLES: "That's impossible."

CAROL: "It is not. It's easy. I'd fill it with holes."

Al Kaufman, The Ben Roth Agency

"That note you sent home to my father—I lost it in the fight I had with a kid who said you're not the prettiest teacher in school."

Book Mark

ANDY: "I've forgotten how far I've read in my book."
SANDY: "Just look for the place where the clean pages start."

Believe It or Not

LIZ: "I bet you I found a word misspelled in the dictionary."
LOU: "Oh, I don't believe it!"
LIZ: "Here it is, 'misspelled.'"

On the Cob

UNCLE GUS: "I imagine that the boys in your school call you by some nickname."
JAKE: "Sure, Uncle Gus, they call me 'corns.'"
UNCLE GUS: "Why on earth do they call you 'corns'?"
JAKE: "Because I'm always at the foot of the class."

Watchful

TEACHER: "Edgar, why do you keep looking at your watch?"
EDGAR: "I was afraid you wouldn't have time to finish this interesting lesson."

QUICK QUIPS

Get the Point?

TED: "How come you were late today?"

NED: "My bike had a flat tire on the way to school. I must have hit something sharp."

TED: "It's your own fault. You know there's a fork in the road on the way to school!"

* * *

MILLIE: "Who was the first person who came from the ark when it landed?"

WILLIE: "Noah."

MILLIE: "No, Willie, you're wrong. Don't you remember that Noah came forth?"

No More?

POP: "Janie, you aren't whispering in class anymore, are you?"

JANIE: "Not any more than I used to."

Saving Plan

MOE: "Did you know that Dick runs to school every day behind the bus to save fifteen cents?"

JOE: "I know how he can save more money every day."

MOE: "How?"

JOE: "He can run behind a taxi and save seventy-five cents."

BOB: "Did you hear what happened to Butch when his bike ran into a brick wall?"

BETSY: "Goodness, no. What did happen?"

BOB: "Butch was knocked speechless and his bike was knocked spokeless."

How's This for Size?

HUGHIE: "Who is bigger? Mrs. Bigger, Mr. Bigger, or the baby?"

LOUIE: "The baby, of course. He's a little Bigger."

Wrong Seat

KITTY: "What was the trouble on the school bus yesterday?"

KENNY: "Some fellow had his eye on a seat and then another boy came and sat on it."

* * *

Little Ozzie came home from his first day at school and told his mother that he was never going back.

"What's the use of school," he said. "I can't read and I can't write, and the teacher won't let me talk."

Mother Knows Best

Henry sat in the back of the room sniffing and rubbing his nose.

Finally the teacher walked over to him and said: "Henry, do you have a handkerchief?"

"Yes," answered Henry, "but my mother says I mustn't lend it to anyone."

No Laughing Matter

SUSY: "Mother, today in the school bus a little girl fell off her seat and everyone laughed except me."

MOTHER: "That was very kind of you, dear. Who was the little girl?"

SUSY: "Me."

* * *

TEACHER: *(To new pupil)* "Are you the oldest in your family?"

NEW PUPIL: "Of course, not. My parents are older."

Heads or . . .

The kindergarten teacher wanted to find out how much her new class knew. She put a fifty-cent piece on her desk, and asked: "Can anyone tell me what this is?"

A small boy in the front row leaned forward, and said quickly, "Tails."

Follow the Leader

MISS SMITH: "Alan, which letter comes after 'A' in the alphabet?"

ALAN: "All of 'em."

SCHOOL DAZE

"Why are you crying, Timmie?"
"Because my brother has a holiday and I haven't."
"How come you don't have a holiday?"
"Because I'm too young to go to school."

Old-Timer

AUNT MAY: "Have you learned to spell yet, Walter?"
WALTER: "Sure."
AUNT MAY: "Let me hear you spell 'kitten'."
WALTER: "I'm getting too old for kitten. Listen to me spell 'cat.'"

Discovery

TEACHER: "Who discovered America, Janet?"
JANET: "A man named Ohio."
TEACHER: "That isn't right. It was Columbus."
JANET: "That's who I meant. Columbus Ohio."

Pay Attention

TEACHER: "What are you reading about, George?"
GEORGE: "I don't know."
TEACHER: "But you were reading aloud."
GEORGE: "Yes, but I wasn't listening."

68

J. Monahan, The Ben Roth Agency

"Before I tell you why I'm late—would you mind turning that picture to the wall?"

MOTHER: "Do you remember any of the nice things you saw on your trip to the museum, Clara?"

CLARA: "Oh, yes, mother."

MOTHER: "Can you tell me what they were called?"

CLARA: "Most of them were named 'hands off.'"

* * *

JANE: (*Entertaining Joe Doaks at dinner with the family*) "Sister, why didn't you put a knife and fork at Joe's place?"

LITTLE SISTER: "Didn't think he needed it. You said he eats like a horse."

* * *

TEACHER: "Why don't you answer me?"

GUS: "I did. I shook my head."

TEACHER: "You didn't expect me to hear it rattle clear up here, did you?"

* * *

MOTHER: "Did you give the goldfish fresh water?"

LITTLE LUCY: "What's the use? They didn't drink what I gave them yesterday."

70

TEACHER: "Alfred, can you define nonsense?"
ALFRED: "Yes, Teacher—an elephant hanging over a cliff with his tail tied to a daisy."

❀ ❀ ❀

TEACHER: *(Rapping on desk)* "Order please!"
SLEEPY VOICE FROM BACK ROW: "Hamburger with onions for me."

❀ ❀ ❀

NICK: "The driver of that car ahead of us must be one of my teachers."
DICK: "Why do you say that?"
NICK: "He's so stubborn about letting us pass."

❀ ❀ ❀

ROGER: "Why can't you throw a dollar across the Delaware River the way George Washington did?"
ROSE: "Because money doesn't go as far as it used to."

❀ ❀ ❀

TEACHER: "Archie, name three collective nouns."
ARCHIE: "Flypaper, wastebasket, and vacuum cleaner."

MOTHER: "Well, Tommy, did you learn much on your first day at school?"

TOMMY: "Not enough. I have to go back tomorrow."

❋ ❋ ❋

ANDY: "Hey, Sandy, aren't you coming out to play?"

SANDY: "No. I have to stay in and help my father with my homework."

❋ ❋ ❋

ALPHABET SOUP

What is invisible, yet never out of sight?
The letter "s".

. . .

What is the happiest letter in the alphabet?
U because it is always in fun.

. . .

How can you say in two letters that you are twice the size of your friend?
I W

. . .

Al Kaufman, The Ben Roth Agency

Why is E the most unlucky letter?
Because it is never in cash, always in debt, and never out of danger.

* * *

Why is the letter R necessary for friendship?
Because without it, your friends would be fiends.

* * *

What is the hottest letter?
B because it makes oil boil.

* * *

Why should your mother never put the letter M in the refrigerator?
Because it changes ice into mice.

* * *

Why is the letter A like twelve o'clock?
Because it comes in the middle of day.

* * *

Why is the letter D like a wedding ring?
Because we cannot be wed without it.

* * *

When are you like the letter B?
When you are in bed.

74

Why is the letter D like a sailor?
Because it follows the C.

* * *

What are the smartest letters in the alphabet?
The Y's (wise).

* * *

What is the difference between here and there?
The letter T.

* * *

I'm last of my race,
But in Zealand, first place.
I'm with a wizard,
But witch I never met.
Of zeal and zest I also brag,
I also love to go zigzag.
The letter Z.

* * *

I'm found in loss,
But never in gain;
If you search there,
'Twill be in vain.
I'm found in hour,
But not in day.
What am I? Can you say?
The letter O.

75

The beginning of eternity,
The end of time and space,
The start of every end,
The end of every place.
The letter E.

* * *

I in vivacity abound,
I'm in vain but never proud,
In the evening I am found,
Mornings I'm never around.
The letter V.

* * *

Now it's the truth,
I am in youth.
When with another,
I mean my brother.
The letter U; with his brother, W.

* * *

BRAIN TEASERS

How many pretty girls in a straight line would it take to reach from New York to Boston, a distance of 232 miles?

Two hundred and thirty-two, because a miss is as good as a mile.

*   *   *

From a word with five letters, take two and leave one.

Al-one.

*   *   *

How many peas in a pint?

One p.

*   *   *

A duck in front of two ducks; a duck behind two ducks; and a duck between two ducks. How many ducks were there in all?

Three ducks.

There were sixteen ears of corn in a barrel. Each night a rabbit came and carried away three ears. How long did it take the rabbit to empty the barrel?
Sixteen nights. One ear of corn and his own two ears carried away each night.

* * *

If a man gives fifteen cents to one of his sons, and a dime to another, what time is it?
A quarter to two.

* * *

If all the money in the world was divided equally among all the people in the world, what would each one get?
An equal share.

* * *

How many cubic feet of earth can you take out of a hole that is three feet square and three feet deep?
None. It has all been taken out.

* * *

There is a girl who works in a candy store in New York. She is six feet tall, her waist measures 42 inches, and she wears a size 10 shoe. What do you think she weighs?
She weighs candy.

What grows in value by one half when you turn it upside down?
The number 6.

* * *

What cannot run although it has three feet?
A yard.

* * *

What is about three inches tall, nine inches long, and four inches wide, and contains a solid foot?
A shoe.

The Evening Standard

"The least you can do is help me with your homework!"

How many soft-boiled eggs can a giant eat on an empty stomach?
One. After that, his stomach is no longer empty.

* * *

What can be divided, but no one can see where it was divided?
Water.

* * *

You see ten dogs running down the street. What time is it?
Nine after one.

* * *

What has eight legs, two arms, three heads, and two wings?
A man riding a horse and carrying a chicken.

* * *

Behind each boy is a girl. Behind each girl is a boy. Now, what is the smallest number of pupils that can be arranged in that manner?
One boy and one girl—back to back.

* * *

My head and tail both equal are,
My middle slender as a bee,

Whether I stand on head or heel,
    Is all the same to you or me.
But if my head should be cut off,
    It's true but very strange,
My head and body cut apart,
    Immediately to nothing change.
The number 8.

*   *   *

What is the difference between a person late for a train and the teacher in a girls' school?
One misses the train; the other trains the misses.

*   *   *

I am very easily destroyed. If you just name me I am demolished. If you speak, even in a whisper, you break me. What am I?
Silence.

*   *   *

Mr. Black insisted that his house face north on all sides. The real estate man had a lot of trouble finding him a house that would have all the windows facing north, and a porch that ran around the house and faced north on all sides.

One day the real estate man came to Mr. Black and said: "I've found just the place to build your house.

But I'm having a little trouble finding out who owns the land so that you can buy it."

Where was the real estate man planning to build Mr. Black's new house?

At the South Pole. That's the only place in the world where every direction is north.

❈ ❈ ❈

CAN YOU GUESS THESE?

A city in China?	*Canton*
A political can?	*Candidate*
A bright can?	*Candle*
A singing can?	*Canary*
A can in Panama?	*Canal*
A noisy can?	*Cannon*
A floating can?	*Canoe*
A sweet can?	*Candy*
An uncivilized can?	*Cannibal*

❈ ❈ ❈

What is the difference between a railroad conductor and a teacher?

One minds the train; the other trains the mind.

❈ ❈ ❈

TRICKY TONGUE TWISTERS

Two timid toads trying to trot to Tarrytown.

❀ ❀ ❀

Three terrible, thumping tigers tickling trout.

❀ ❀ ❀

Five frivolous foreigners fleeing from ferocious foxes.

❀ ❀ ❀

Six Scottish soldiers successfully shooting snipe.

❀ ❀ ❀

Seven serious Southerners setting sail for Switzerland.

❀ ❀ ❀

Six thick thistle sticks.

❀ ❀ ❀

Ten tremendous tomcats tottering on the tops of three tall trees.

Flesh of fresh flying fish.

* * *

Twelve tired tailors thoughtfully twisting twine.

* * *

Eleven enormous elephants elegantly eating Easter eggs.

* * *

A bitter biting bittern,
Bit a better brother bittern
And the bitter better bittern bit the bitter biter back.
And the bitter bittern, bitten
By the better bitten bittern,
Said: "I'm a bitter biter bit, alas!"

* * *

MUSIC MAYHEM

What musical instrument must you never believe?
The lyre.

❋ ❋ ❋

What's the most popular tune?
Fortune.

❋ ❋ ❋

If you take away the first letter, it will make you
sick. What's the word?
Music.

❋ ❋ ❋

What is the most honest musical instrument?
An upright piano.

❋ ❋ ❋

Why is a pianist like a prison guard?
Because they both finger the keys.

BABS: *(Talking about the pretty new neighbor girl)* "She must be very musical."
MABS: "How can you tell?"
BABS: "By the cords in her neck."

* * *

MINNIE: "What do you mean when you say my brother is a 'waterproof' singer?"
MOE: "I mean nobody can drown him out."

* * *

SINGER: "Did you notice how my voice filled the hall last night?"
MUSIC CRITIC: "Yes, and I saw several people leave to make room for it."

* * *

MOTHER: "I don't think the neighbors like Tommy's music."
FATHER: "Why?"
MOTHER: "Today they gave him a sharp knife and asked him if he knew what was inside his drum."

Sour Note

The convicts have a band,
It's as bad as it can be;
They're familiar with the bars,
But cannot get the key.

* * *

HAPPY HISTORY AND JOLLY GEOGRAPHY

What was the name of Washington's valet?
Valley Forge

❀ ❀ ❀

Where did Caesar go on his thirty-ninth birthday?
Into his fortieth year.

❀ ❀ ❀

Why is Henry VIII different from other husbands?
First he married his wives, then he axed them.

❀ ❀ ❀

Why did William Tell shudder when he shot an apple from his son's head?
Because it was an arrow escape.

❀ ❀ ❀

Why is the letter P like a Roman emperor?
Because it is near O.

What is the fruit of history?
Dates.

* * *

Why is a barefoot boy like an Eskimo?
Because he wears no shoes (snow shoes).

* * *

Where were the first doughnuts fried?
In Greece.

* * *

What islands should be good singers?
The Canary Islands.

* * *

What is the best land for infants?
Lapland.

* * *

What is found only in the very center of America
and Australia?
The letter R.

* * *

Who are the fastest people on earth?
The Russians.

Why is an island like the letter T?
Because it is in the middle of water.

* * *

What islands are good to eat?
The Sandwich Islands.

* * *

Why is Asia like the meat department of a super‑market?
Because there's Turkey in it.

Bernhardt, Successful Farming

"Not 'I have sawed a chair,' Johnny—I saw a chair, or I have seen a chair—"

* * *

Mystery

He asked me, "When?"
I could not tell.
He queried, "Who?"
Again I fell.
He named a man—
To me a stranger,
And I could see myself in danger.
What was this plight—this mystery?
Oh, just my course in history!

❖ ❖ ❖

ALEC: "Can you name the capital of every state in one minute?"
ALVIN: "No, can you?"
ALEC: "Sure. Washington, D.C.

❖ ❖ ❖

LOU: "What would you do if you found Chicago Ill?"
STU: "Call the Baltimore M.D."

❖ ❖ ❖

In the Egyptian room of the museum, Gus and Gert stopped before a mummy in a mummy case bearing a card which read: 2453 B.C.

"What do you suppose 2453 B.C. means?" whispered Gert.

"I don't know," replied Gus. "Unless it's the license number of the car that hit him."

* * *

JACK: "I know the name of the capital of North Carolina."

JILL: "Really?"

JACK: "No, Raleigh."

* * *

FRED: "What do Abraham Lincoln and Dwight Eisenhower have in common?"

TED: "A Gettysburg address."

SOME DIFFICULT FEATS (FEETS)

1. What is a foot to get for a barefoot boy?

2. What foot tells you that someone is right behind you?

3. What foot do you find on a page?

4. What foot do you find on a stage?

5. What is a foot that steals things?

6. What foot do you feel after a long walk?

7. What foot is a servant in a castle?

8. What foot does grandma like to have in the living room?

9. What foot is free and a roamer?

10. What foot is an exciting outdoor game?

---

1. Footwear 2. Football 3. Footnote 4. Footlight 5. Footpad 6. Footsore 7. Footman 8. Footstool 9. Footloose 10. Football